FOOD and FARMING

FARMING in the FUTURE

Ian Graham

WAYLAND

First published in 2009 by Wayland

Copyright © Wayland 2009

Wayland
338 Euston Road
London NW1 3BH

Wayland Australia
Level 17/207 Kent Street
Sydney, NSW 2000

Produced for Wayland by Discovery Books Ltd.

Editor: Julia Adams
Managing Editor, Discovery Books: Rachel Tisdale
Editor, Discovery Books: Jenny Vaughan
Designer and illustrator: Graham Rich
Picture researcher: Bobby Humphrey
Consultant: Nicholas Rowles

British Library Cataloguing in Publication Data
Graham, Ian, 1953-
Farming in the future. - (Food and farming)
1. Agriculture - Forecasting - Juvenile literature
I. Title
630.1'12

ISBN: 978 0 7502 5699 5

Printed in China

Wayland is a division of Hachette Children's Books,
an Hachette UK company.

www.hachettelivre.co.uk

Picture credits
Getty Images: pp. 5 & cover bottom (Imagemore Co.,
Ltd.), 7 (Jim Watson/AFP), 11 (Mitch Kezar), 19
(Frederic J. Brown), 22 (Randy Olson/National
Geographic), 26 (Dorling Kindersley), 27 (Matt Cardy),
29 (George Frey); Istockphoto.com: pp. 21, 23 (Mark
Higgins), 25 (Pattie Steib); Novariant: pp. 12, 13;
Science Photo Library: pp. 16 (Matt Meadows, Peter
Arnold Inc.), 28 (NASA); Shutterstock: pp. 8 (Shao
Weiwei), 10 (Jens Stolt), 20 (sgame); University of
Warwick: p. 14; Vision Robotics Corporation: p. 15

CONTENTS

THE CHANGING WORLD OF FARMING

Within the next few years, farming methods in much of the world will almost certainly change. This must happen in order to meet the challenge of making sure that everyone on earth has enough to eat.

A new Green Revolution

People first started worrying about whether farms would be able to produce enough food for everyone as long as 200 years ago. By the middle of the 20th century, science and technology seemed to have come to the rescue with solutions to the world's food shortages. Scientists created new kinds of crops that produced more food, along with chemicals to make them grow strongly and other chemicals to kill pests and weeds. This increased the food supply so much that it was called the Green Revolution. But there is still a need for improvement, so a new Green Revolution is now needed to carry on feeding everyone throughout the 21st century.

The need for change

There are several reasons why farming is changing. The world's population is expected to grow from 6.5 billion today to about 9 billion by 2050. Farms will have to provide food for all the extra people. The growing population will need more land for housing, work and transport, leaving less for farming. In addition, the world's climate seems to be changing. There will probably be more and longer droughts in some places and more severe storms and floods in others, making farming more difficult. Scientists may be able to solve some of these problems by using genetic science (altering the makeup of food crops), computers, wireless communications, the Internet, robots and space technology. However, some people think that, instead, we should go back to a more natural way of growing our food.

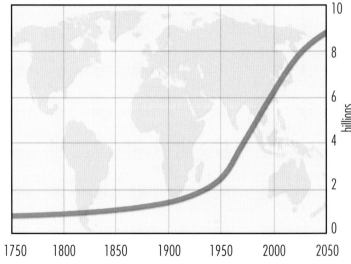

WORLD POPULATION INCREASE SINCE 1750

▲ *The world's population is increasing fast. There are now almost nine times more people on earth than there were 200 years ago, and numbers are set to grow further.*

▲ *Many genetically modified crops are still at an experimental stage.*
Here, a scientist examines a trial crop of GM strawberries.

CASE STUDY

Seed banks

There are about 1,400 collections of seeds stored in seed banks around the world. These are vital because, if we preserve the different sorts of plants we have today, we keep open the opportunity to use them to breed new kinds of crops in the future. One of the most important seed banks is the Svalbard Global Seed Vault. It is built inside a mountain on the Norwegian island of Spitsbergen. It can store up to 2.25 billion seeds at -18°C. At this temperature, seeds can survive for hundreds of years.

THE THREAT OF CLIMATE CHANGE

Most scientists agree that the world is warming up. They believe this is because of a rise in gases produced by human activities. These gases enter the atmosphere and trap warmth from the sun. This is called the greenhouse effect.

Farming in a drier world

If the world's temperature rises, long droughts are likely to become more common in some places. Australia and Africa are already experiencing this. Australia's worst drought in a century began in 2002 and had not fully ended by 2008. New kinds of wheat, maize and other crops could be bred to survive these conditions. One study suggests that hotter, drier conditions in southern Africa could mean the region will lose more than 30 per cent of its main crop, maize, by 2030.

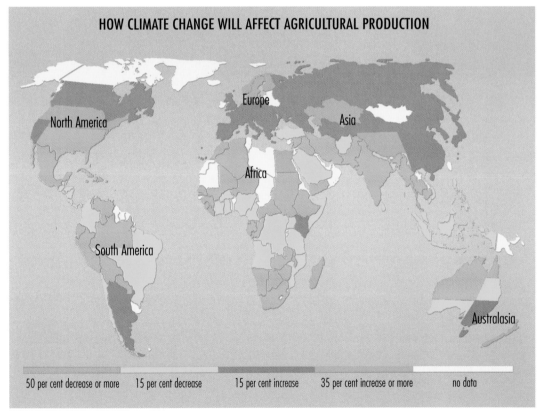

HOW CLIMATE CHANGE WILL AFFECT AGRICULTURAL PRODUCTION

North America

Europe

Asia

Africa

South America

Australasia

50 per cent decrease or more   15 per cent decrease   15 per cent increase   35 per cent increase or more   no data

◀ *This map shows how scientists expect agricultural production over the world to change by 2080. While production may rise in cooler parts of the world, regions such as Africa and Asia will be very badly affected.*

Losing soil

When soil is dry and cleared of trees, the problem of soil erosion (when soil is washed away by rain, or blown away by the wind) is made worse. The world already loses 10 million hectares of crop land every year because of erosion. That is an area of land equal to South Korea or Iceland. Farmers can reduce this risk by never leaving soil bare of plants. They can grow plants such as clover between the main crops, to help to hold the soil together. Farmers can also work in organic material such as animal waste. This helps the soil to hold water better.

SOIL EROSION WORLDWIDE

Every year, an area ten times the size of the UK is made so barren it cannot produce food, all as a result of erosion by wind and rain. The best soil is topsoil, which contains the nutrients crops need to grow. In one third of the world's croplands, topsoil is eroding faster than it can be replaced. It takes many years for topsoil to replace itself naturally, and repairing such damage is expensive. In the US, topsoil loss costs around $125 billion per year.

▲ *Drought can kill crops and devastate farms. Farmers may be left bankrupt and local and even international food shortages become worse.*

IRRIGATION AND RAINWATER

By the year 2030, there will be another 2.5 billion people on earth. They will need water, and farms will need more water to produce food for them. Where will it come from?

Irrigation and rainwater

Water for farms comes from rain and irrigation. Irrigation is artificial watering, using rivers, lakes and underground water sources. Scientists think irrigation could supply about a quarter of the extra water needed by farms in the future.

The rest must come from rainfall. We cannot make more rain, but we can make better use of what we have. Two-thirds of the rain that falls on farmland evaporates, runs into rivers or sinks into the ground. Farms will have to find ways to catch and use more of this wasted water.

▲ *This desalination plant in Dubai provides fresh water in a region where fresh water from other sources is especially scarce.*

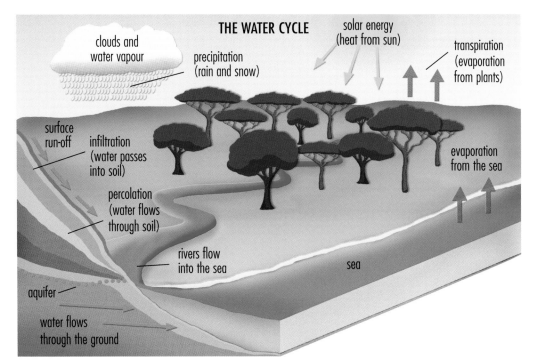

THE WATER CYCLE

clouds and water vapour

precipitation (rain and snow)

solar energy (heat from sun)

transpiration (evaporation from plants)

surface run-off

infiltration (water passes into soil)

percolation (water flows through soil)

evaporation from the sea

rivers flow into the sea

sea

aquifer

water flows through the ground

◀ *When rain falls, much of it runs into rivers, or into the ground, and eventually into the sea. Plants take up some rainwater and give off water vapour, along with the water vapour from the sea, land and rivers. In this way, plants play a part in the water cycle.*

Ditches and drains catch water that runs off fields. Porous membranes (sheets) on the ground help to stop water evaporating. Future farms will store saved rainwater in giant water tanks or reservoirs. We may also all have to adapt to using less water, for example, by eating less meat. It takes about 750 litres of water to produce a kilogram of wheat, but up to 100,000 litres to produce a kilogram of beef.

Using seawater

Nearly all the world's water is salty seawater. It cannot be used for watering crops or given to animals to drink. However, it can be changed to fresh water by desalination (removing the salt). Desalination is expensive, but some countries, such as Israel, Singapore, China, India and Australia already do this. So do the states of California, Arizona, Texas and Florida in the US.

CASE STUDY

Desalination in Israel

In the 1990s, Israel's government decided to build a line of desalination plants along its coast to help with the country's water shortage. The first of these, at Ashkelon, is the biggest of its type in the world. It produces 100 million cubic metres of fresh water from the sea every year: about six per cent of Israel's total water needs.

USING THE INTERNET

Farms in rich countries are businesses and, like all businesses, use the Internet. Farmers depend on it to keep up to date with farming news and communicate by email. They are likely to find new ways of using the Internet in the future.

Making maps

A future Internet farm may use devices called sensors, spread all over the farm. These collect information about the weather and soil conditions, so no-one has to go out to the fields and measure anything. Sensors detect changes and make measurements, which they change to electrical signals. They send these to a computer, which combines all the information with weather reports and crop information downloaded from the Internet to create maps and graphs. These show the farmer what the conditions in the fields are like today, and predict how they

◄ *This weather sensor on a Spanish vineyard helps the landowner find out exactly what conditions are in this part of the farm, without having to go there to measure it.*

▲ *Farmers used to have to go out to their fields to collect information from sensors. This is no longer necessary, as the information can be transmitted by radio.*

are likely to change in the next week or month. The farmer can use the information to help plan work in the fields better. Systems like this will let farmers check their fields and crops at any time of the day or night without getting their boots dirty!

Trying it out

In a trial of this type of computerised system, sensors have been placed all over a vineyard in Sonoma County, California, in the US. The sensors measure wind speed, humidity (the amount of moisture in the air) and the temperature of the soil and air. They send the information to a receiver in the vineyard, which sends it on to a laboratory, where it is used to create reports and maps. These are put on the Internet for farmers to look at.

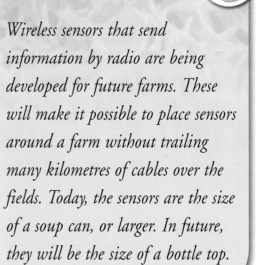

RADIO CONTACT

Wireless sensors that send information by radio are being developed for future farms. These will make it possible to place sensors around a farm without trailing many kilometres of cables over the fields. Today, the sensors are the size of a soup can, or larger. In future, they will be the size of a bottle top.

PRECISION FARMING

Crops take nutrients and minerals out of the soil, and farmers must put these back to make it fertile again. If farmers can find out exactly where most fertilisers and other chemicals are needed, they can save money. This is called precision farming.

Testing soil

Arable farms (farms where crops are grown) are beginning to make use of the satellite technology that car drivers use. Farmers use it to record where the soil is most fertile. Samples of soil are taken from different parts of a field, and its position in the field is recorded by using GPS (Global Positioning System) satellites. The measurements are fed into a computer, which produces a map that shows which parts of a field need most fertiliser. Photographs taken from an aircraft or spacecraft show the differences in crop growth in different parts of a field, along with the effects of pests and diseases.

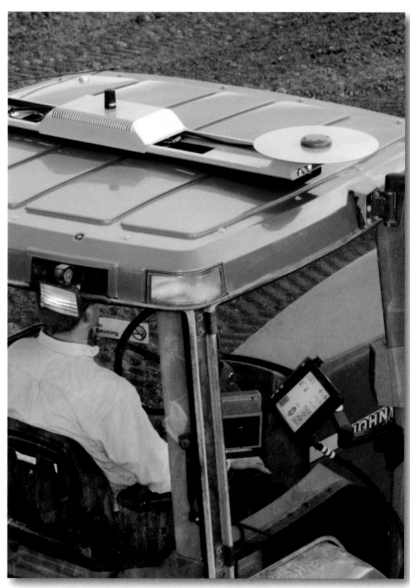

▶ *GPS receivers are used to help farmers know which areas of land need special attention.*

SATELLITES

The Global Positioning System (GPS) is a fleet of 24 satellites orbiting the earth. They send out radio signals. A GPS receiver on the ground, for instance in a farm field, can use these signals to work out exactly where it is.

Speeding up

The most advanced tractors and combine harvesters are fitted with computers. These contain GPS receivers, which can give farmers information even faster than taking photographs from the air or space. They will make it possible for farmers to know the locations of problems such as poor crop growth. As a vehicle crosses a field, its computer records problems such as poor growth. The GPS unit tells the computer where the problems are. Then, when the farmer applies fertiliser, the computer makes sure that each part of the field receives the correct amount. Precision farming may become the standard way to farm in the future, but only for farmers in rich countries, who can afford the technology.

▶ *This farm tractor is fitted with satellite navigation equipment, to steer the tractor around fields in the most efficient way.*

ROBOT FARMERS

In 2003, for the first time in history, more people were living in the world's towns and cities than in the countryside. Fewer people than ever are working on the land, yet farmers must find ways of producing enough food for everyone.

Robots to the rescue

Machines like combine harvesters enable fewer people to do more work than was possible in the past, but they still need human operators. Employing people can be expensive, but future farms could cut costs by using robots, which are machines that work by themselves. This would mean employing even fewer people. Robots have been used in factories since the 1960s. They move materials and parts around and do jobs like painting, welding, cutting and assembly. In future, robots will also work on farms.

HARD WORKERS

The farm robots built so far work more slowly than people, but the robots do not have to stop for lunch or when it gets dark. They can work 24 hours a day if there is enough work for them to do. Some of them can even contact the farmer if they find a problem!

◀ *In this picture, a robotic mushroom picker is being tried out at the University of Warwick. It uses a camera to select only mushrooms of the exact size needed, and then picks them using a suction cup.*

Farming robots are already being developed in some agricultural research centres. Robots may one day replace many manned vehicles and machines used on today's farms.

Coping with nature

In factories, robots handle parts that are all the same shape and size, positioned exactly where the robot estimates they will be. Nature is different, and the jobs that robots do are more complicated. They have to deal with fruits of different sizes growing on bushes or trees of different shapes, standing on bumpy ground, with their branches moving in the breeze. Fruit-picking robots need cameras to find the fruit and guide their mechanical hands towards them. They have to grip fruit just tightly enough to pick it without squashing it. Robotics companies and universities are designing farm robots to pick oranges, apples and grapes. The University of Warwick, in England, has built a robot that can pick mushrooms. Other robots, already developed, can cut grass and there are some that can milk cows.

▼ *This is a computer-generated picture of a robot for picking oranges. The idea is that it first scans the trees within a grove, and uses special cameras to create a 3D image of an entire orange tree. It then tells the arms where to find the oranges and to pick them.*

GENETICALLY MODIFIED CROPS

Living things are made of cells. Inside each cell, there are genes, which carry a set of instructions. These are set out in a pattern called the genetic code that tells the cell how to grow. Scientists can change the code. This is called genetic modification.

GM crops

Scientists hope that GM (genetically modified) crops will produce more food, or survive better in harsh conditions. Some may stay fresh longer, or will be resistant to pests, or will not be damaged by weed-killing chemicals. But there are problems. Often, farmers have to buy both the GM seeds and chemicals from the same company, which can be expensive. Also, GM crops may cross-breed with related weeds and breed super weeds. These could be difficult to kill, or they could be plants that insects and other wild animals cannot eat. Some people also worry that GM crops could cause health problems in humans.

GM animals

The genetic code of animals can be changed too, to make them produce more meat or milk, for example. Also, cells can be taken from one animal and grown into a new but identical animal. This is called cloning. However, creating better farm animals in these ways is difficult and expensive, and many people do not want to eat meat from such animals. It is likely that farm animals will be produced in the natural way for the foreseeable future.

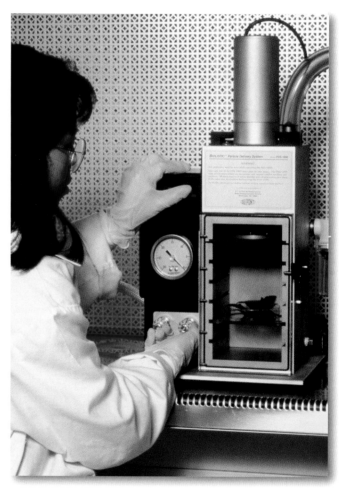

▲ *A scientist operates a 'gene gun' to alter a plant's genes. This is a first step to breeding a GM crop.*

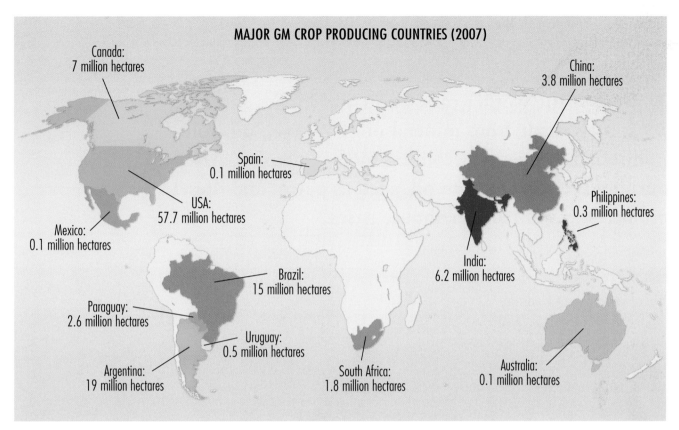

MAJOR GM CROP PRODUCING COUNTRIES (2007)

Canada:
7 million hectares

China:
3.8 million hectares

Spain:
0.1 million hectares

USA:
57.7 million hectares

Philippines:
0.3 million hectares

Mexico:
0.1 million hectares

India:
6.2 million hectares

Brazil:
15 million hectares

Paraguay:
2.6 million hectares

Uruguay:
0.5 million hectares

Australia:
0.1 million hectares

Argentina:
19 million hectares

South Africa:
1.8 million hectares

▲ *This map shows the 13 major GM crop producing countries of the world.
The main GM crops grown are soya beans, maize and cotton. The area of land
used to grow GM crops increased by 12.3 million hectares between 2006 and 2007.*

DEBATE

Are GM crops a good idea?

*More than 10 million farmers on about 120 million hectares of land in 23 countries are
already growing GM crops. This is an area more than twice the size of France, and it is
growing by over 10 million hectares a year. GM seeds are expensive, and some people fear
such plants could damage our health and possibly the environment. However, many farmers
want to grow GM crops because they can be useful. For example, a test crop of drought
resistant maize plants in South Africa produced up to 50 per cent more corn than ordinary
maize in the same dry conditions. Is it right to oppose GM if it can be useful?*

Most of the world's cars, buses and lorries run on fuels made from mineral oil. However, oil from traditional sources is becoming more expensive. Also, burning fuels made from oil, such as petrol and diesel, produces unwanted greenhouse gases.

Fuel crops

There are ways of making cleaner fuel. One is to make fuels called biofuels, from plants. For example, corn, palm, soya beans, wheat and sugar cane can be processed to produce ethanol. This can be made from ordinary oil, but when it is made from plants, it is called bioethanol. It can be burned in car engines, and in aircrafts' jet engines. The world leader in biofuel production is Brazil. Most new cars in Brazil use bioethanol mixed with petrol. Other countries, including the US, Australia and Sweden, are beginning to use petrol/biofuel mixtures too.

▶ *This diagram shows the stages of making ethanol from plant matter. Although a whole range of plant crops can be used, recently, crops have been grown especially for this purpose.*

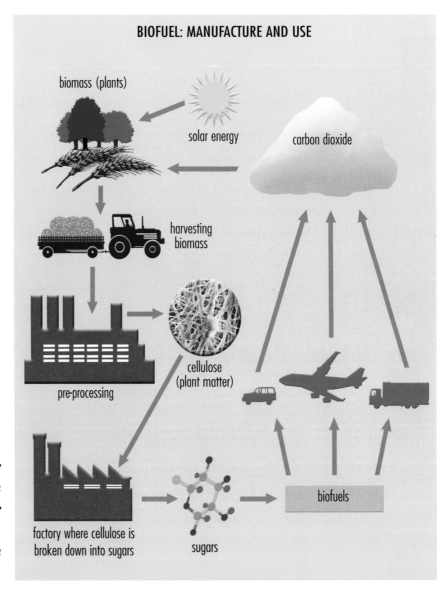

BIOFUEL: MANUFACTURE AND USE

biomass (plants)

solar energy

carbon dioxide

harvesting biomass

pre-processing

cellulose (plant matter)

factory where cellulose is broken down into sugars

sugars

biofuels

▲ *This picture shows a maize crop in China. Maize is an important food in much of the world, and using it to make fuel could mean that many people would suffer by not having enough to eat.*

Rising prices

Brazilian biofuel is made from sugar cane. In other places, some farmers have started using food crops such as wheat or maize to make biofuel. This can create problems. A report by the World Bank found that using wheat and maize to make fuel, instead of growing it for food, may have forced food prices up by as much as 75 per cent between 2002 and 2008. Governments are now re-thinking the use of biofuels. In the future, biofuels may be made from waste materials such as wood chips, corncobs or waste from fruit farming, so that they do not affect food prices.

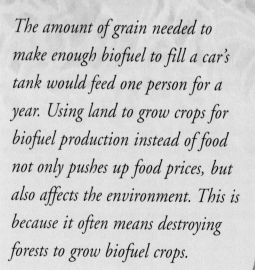

PROBLEMS WITH BIOFUEL

The amount of grain needed to make enough biofuel to fill a car's tank would feed one person for a year. Using land to grow crops for biofuel production instead of food not only pushes up food prices, but also affects the environment. This is because it often means destroying forests to grow biofuel crops.

NANOTECHNOLOGY

A new technology called nanotechnology is being used to make stronger, lighter materials and surfaces that stay clean and dry by themselves. In future, farmers may use nanotechnology to grow healthier crops, while also using smaller amounts of chemicals.

Tiny but mighty

Nano means one billionth. A nanometre is one billionth of a metre long. Nanotechnology deals with nanoparticles. These are particles and parts no bigger than about 100 nanometres, which are too small to see without a microscope. Scientists all over the world are busy studying how to use nanoparticles in all sorts of products and industries, including farming. Specks of chemicals as small as nanoparticles take part in chemical reactions faster and more completely than normal powders. This makes the chemical more powerful. Farm chemicals in the form of nanoparticles could be used in smaller quantities than normal farm chemicals. Hollow nanoparticles filled with chemicals can be designed to release the chemicals over a period of time. Instead of a crop being sprayed with big doses of chemicals, the nanoparticles could release chemicals into the soil slowly over a longer time. Other nanoparticles could be designed to release their chemicals only in certain conditions, such as when they get wet, or at a certain temperature or when particular substances are present in the soil.

◀ *This is a magnified picture of a nanotube. Miniscule tubes like this could one day be used by farmers to detect the levels of chemicals such as insecticides and other pesticides in the soil.*

Using nanotechnology today

Nanotechnology is already used in more than 600 products on sale today, including sun creams, paints and self-cleaning window glass. When used in farming, it could reduce costs as well as the amount of chemicals used. However, people opposed to nanotechnology say that more research must be done into the effects of nanoparticles on the soil and on the plants and the people who eat crops treated with nanoparticles.

▼ *This farmer is spraying crops to kill pests. Nanotechnology could mean using a smaller quantity of chemicals, which may have less impact on the environment.*

HOW SMALL?

The nanoparticles that scientists plan to use in farming are so small that a line of 800 of them would be as long as the thickness of a human hair. A line of 10,000 of these nanoparticles would be just one millimetre long!

FINDING NEW FOODS

We eat a tiny fraction of all the available plants and animals on earth. Only 30 or so plant species are sold for food, and the meat most of us eat comes from just a handful of animals.

Eating bugs

In future, farmers may grow a wider variety of crops and animals, to increase the food supply. Insects, which are hardly ever eaten in western countries, can be a surprisingly good source of nutrients. Even though they do not seem to have much meat on them, they can be more nutritious than the same weight of beef or fish, and they are popular foods in some parts of the world. People in more than 100 countries eat about 2,000 species of insects. Caterpillars, termites and locusts are eaten in Africa. Grasshoppers are enjoyed in Japan. Witchetty grubs are a delicacy among Australian Aborigines, and crickets are farmed in Thailand and exported to surrounding countries.

▲ *Thai fishermen unload a catch of jellyfish, which will be sold as food.*

Future farms

Making more widespread use of less popular plants and creatures could increase the world's food supply, but people would have to get used to eating unusual foods. Sometimes, science can help. People are often put off by the thought of putting something with a head and legs in their mouth. Dutch researchers are working on a project to produce insect cells on their own, with no head or legs. Perhaps they could be shaped into insect burgers. We may have to get used to eating seaweeds and sea creatures such as jellyfish. In Asia, fishermen catch 450,000 tonnes of jellyfish for food each year. We already have fish farms. Perhaps we will have insect farms, snake farms or offshore seaweed and jellyfish farms in the future.

CASE STUDY

Mopane worms

Mopane worms are the caterpillars of the emperor moth. They can be up to 10 cm long. They are a favourite snack throughout southern Africa. The caterpillars are collected, their guts squeezed out, and then they are dried. About 1,600 tonnes of dried mopane worms are sold in South Africa every year.

▲ *Snake meat is popular in much of Asia, and many people believe it can protect them from catching colds.*

SKYSCRAPER FARMS

The distance food travels from farms to shops is measured in food miles. Many people think that food miles should be reduced to cut the greenhouse gas emissions from the trucks, ships and planes that transport food around the world.

Local food

One idea is to build future farms in cities. Scientists at Columbia University in New York believe that these need not use any more space than an ordinary skyscraper. Skyscrapers with big glass windows are like tall greenhouses. In future, some skyscrapers might have crops inside them instead of offices. These could grow all year, away from bad weather and protected from pests outside. Crops could grow in gravel instead of soil, using a method called hydroponics. Water containing nutrients flows through the gravel and the plants take it up. Farms in skyscrapers are called vertical farms. They use land very efficiently. A single vertical farm could feed between 10,000 and 35,000 people.

MAXIMISING SPACE

Scientists think that each floor of a vertical farm could grow around four times as much produce as the same area of land out of doors. This means that a vertical farm 58 floors high could grow as much food as a traditional farm covering more than 200 times as much land.

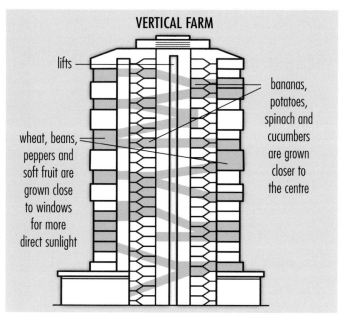

VERTICAL FARM

lifts

wheat, beans, peppers and soft fruit are grown close to windows for more direct sunlight

bananas, potatoes, spinach and cucumbers are grown closer to the centre

▲ *The green bands show the planting areas in a vertical farm. Crops are grown in positions that suit their individual needs for direct sunlight best.*

▲ *Salad crops are especially suited to hydroponic systems. Many of them need large amounts of water, and grow well without soil.*

Powering up

Producing food indoors usually needs a lot of electricity for heating, fans, lighting, watering systems and so on. This is mainly made by burning coal or gas in power stations, which produces greenhouse gases. Vertical farms will avoid this problem by using a combination of solar energy, wind turbines and burning waste from the crops. This is cleaner and more environmentally friendly than traditional forms of energy. Even though burning waste plants gives out carbon dioxide, a greenhouse gas, each crop takes in carbon dioxide from the air as it grows. Although it returns this to the air when it is burned, it does not make global warming any worse. It is said to be carbon neutral.

BACK TO NATURE?

Some people believe that the best way forward in farming is to use a more natural way of producing food. This means stopping the use of chemicals and technology to produce the most food possible from every square metre of land.

Intensive farming: the problems

Using chemicals and technology to produce as much food as possible is called intensive farming. People who are opposed to it say it destroys the plants and creatures that live naturally in the soil and help it to become fertile. Another disadvantage is that the fertilisers and other chemicals used in intensive farming can get into rivers, where they pollute the water and kill fish and other small creatures.

Finding another way

When farmers work organically, they do not use factory-made chemicals, and this saves them money. Organic farming is hard work but it can be profitable. It is especially worthwhile in poor countries. Low-till farming, which uses less ploughing and digging, is also effective, as farmers use their tractors and other machines less. It can mean they burn up to 70 per cent less fuel, which reduces costs, air pollution and greenhouse gas emissions. Between harvests, a catch crop is planted to hold the soil together and prevent soil erosion. It also takes nitrogen from the air and adds it to the soil for the next main crop to use. The crop is then killed and the next main crop is planted through the rotting plants. The rotting plants keep the soil moist and work as a natural fertiliser.

◄ *Organic fruit and vegetables, such as these apples, often look less perfect than those grown using modern fertilisers and pesticides. However, many people believe organic products are safer and tastier.*

DEBATE

Can organic farming provide the answer?

In rich countries, organic farms tend to be less productive than non-organic ones, but their methods are more sustainable. Costs such as fertilisers and pesticides are lower, and there is less damage to the environment. Some research suggests that, in poor countries, organic farming is more productive than farming that uses large amounts of chemicals. However, rising human populations may force us to find more intensive ways of growing food.

▲ *This farmer rears organic turkeys in England. Farming animals organically means rearing them out of doors in as natural conditions as possible and using no artificial chemicals.*

GROWING FOOD IN SPACE

Astronauts could be flying to Mars within the next 50 years. Their missions will be several years long. They will not be able to take enough food for such long missions, so they will have to grow food in space.

Martian farmers

Rather than carry all the food they need, it would be useful for astronauts to grow some. Experiments carried out in the Space Shuttle and International Space Station show that plants can grow successfully inside spacecraft. The next step is to learn how to grow plants for food on Mars.

The ideal plants would be short, so they don't take up much room, have few parts that can't be eaten, grow well in low light and resist diseases. They must also grow well in low gravity on Mars, or in weightless conditions in space on the way to Mars. Plants being tested for this journey include wheat, rice, lettuce, tomatoes and potatoes.

CASE STUDY

Mars in Canada

A research centre at the University of Guelph in Canada uses 24 special chambers for experiments in space farming for several space agencies. The temperature, air pressure, gases and other conditions inside some of the chambers can be changed to copy conditions on the moon or Mars.

▲ *Here, wheat is being grown experimentally in space. Eventually, this type of farming may become an essential part of space missions.*

▲ *These plants are growing at the University of Utah's Mars Desert Research Station. The plants live on waste and water from the research station.*

Give and take

Green plants take in the carbon dioxide astronauts breathe out. They combine it with water and minerals to make food, and give out oxygen, which astronauts need to breathe. In return, some of the minerals the plants need can be extracted from the astronauts' body waste. Space plant research may be useful here on earth. Ever since space exploration began, inventions and discoveries made by space scientists have been used in medicine, industry, business, electronics and communications. Inventions and discoveries made in one kind of research that are used somewhere else are called spin-offs. Spin-offs from space farming could help to improve farming efficiency in general.

GLOSSARY

aquifer a layer of rocks under the ground through which water flows.

arable farm a farm where plant crops are the main source of income for the farmer, rather than animals (livestock).

bankrupt a person or organisation who declared by the law, is unable to pay their debts.

biofuel any fuel made from recently-living plants, rather than ones that died out millions of years ago to form oil or coal. A biofuel called ethanol can be burned in car engines.

carbon neutral an activity that neither adds to nor takes away from the amount of carbon dioxide in the air.

climate the average weather in an area over a long time.

desalination making fresh water from salty seawater.

drought a long period of dry weather.

evaporation when a liquid gradually changes to vapour or into a gas.

fertiliser a substance that makes the soil better able to produce crops.

food miles the distance between the farm where food is grown and the shops where it is sold. It is measured in miles, never kilometres.

gene the very tiny part of the cell of a living thing that tells it how it will grow and develop. Genes are made up of a substance called deoxyribonucleic acid (DNA).

genetic code the way the DNA is organised in genes, so that they can work properly.

genetic modification (GM) altering the genes of a living thing in a way that would not occur in nature.

genetic science the study of genes and genetics.

Global Positioning System (GPS) a fleet of satellites orbiting the earth and sending out radio signals. A receiver on the ground can use these radio signals to calculate its own exact position and work out the way to go to reach a destination.

global warming a rise in the average temperature of the air around the earth, which most climate scientists think is caused by greenhouse gases produced by human activities.

gravity the force that pulls everything down towards the centre of the earth.

greenhouse effect the way that heat from the sun is trapped in the atmosphere by certain gases as it is reflected back from the surface of the earth.

greenhouse gases carbon dioxide and other gases in the air, such as, methane and water vapour, that contribute to the greenhouse effect.

hydroponics a way of growing plants in water with nutrients dissolved in it, instead of in soil.

intensive farming producing a large amount of food from the land, usually by using chemicals and technology.

irrigation watering land by artificial methods. These can be anything from traditional methods such as diverting river water or carrying water to crops in buckets, to modern methods such as mechanical sprinklers.

nanometre a length equal to one billionth of a metre.

nanoparticles tiny particles of substances, less than 100 nanometres long, used in nanotechnology.

nanotechnology a branch of science and engineering concerned with materials, particles and devices no bigger than about 100 nanometres (one ten-thousandth of a millimetre).

nutrients substances that provide nourishment.

organic farming producing food without the use of artificial chemicals.

pesticides chemicals that kill pests, such as destructive insects.

pollution a substance or substances in air, water, soil or food that cause a damaging or unwanted effect.

seed bank a place where plant seeds of many kinds are stored safely, so that they can survive even when the plants they come from have become rare or have disappeared from the rest of the world.

sensor a device that detects a change in something (such as temperature or wind speed) and produces an electrical signal as a response to this.

solar energy the heat and light that comes from the sun.

tropical a place near the equator (the imaginary line around the middle of the earth), where the climate is usually warm all year.

World Bank an international organisation that helps countries in their process of economic development, with loans, advice and research.

TOPIC WEB/FIND OUT MORE

THE FUTURE

Science and Technology
- Debate animal cloning in farming in the future.
- Plan a talk about the importance of seed banks in preserving crop species.
- Find out about satellite positioning and navigation and make a diagram to show how it works.
- Research and list the difficulties of farming on the moon or Mars.

English and Literacy
- Write a description of how farmers in Australia are affected by the ongoing drought, which is the worst in a century.
- Look out for articles in newspapers about farm life on both intensive and organic farms. Are the writers trying get you to support their point of view about farming?

Geography
- Plan a talk on the effects of future climate change on agriculture in different parts of the world.
- Discuss the effects that future population growth might have on farming and the environment in different parts of the world, and people's changing attitudes to land clearance.

Art and Culture
- Find out about traditional art forms that show agriculture, such as paintings from ancient Egypt. Try making similar pictures to show farming today and in the future.
- Collect folk songs and rhymes about farming in the past and adapt them to suit farming in the future.
- Create posters to show how we might use alternative forms of energy to keep food costs down.

History and Economics
- Make a time line to show how the coming of industrialisation and the growth in trade across the world affected food production. What might the future look like on your line?
- Research the risks to the security of food supply. What can we learn about past problems in getting food supplies from abroad, such as during World War II?

FIND OUT MORE

Books

Climate Change (Can The Earth Cope?), by Richard Spilsbury, Wayland, 2008.

Earth SOS (Food For Everyone), by Brenda Walpole, Franklin Watts, 2008.

Genetic Engineering (Ethical Debates), by Pete Moore, Wayland, 2007.

GM Foods (Your Environment), by Jen Green, Franklin Watts, 2007.

Water Supplies (Action For The Environment), by Jude Welton, Franklin Watts, 2006.

Web links

http://www.verticalfarm.com/Designs.aspx See what future vertical farms might look like.

http://ga.water.usgs.gov/edu/mearth.html This website is about water, where it is and where it goes.

http://www.csiro.au/science/Water.html This is an Australian site about water and the country's dry environment.

http://nationalzoo.si.edu/Publications/ZooGoer/2005 /4/edibleinsects.cfm Find out more about insects as food.

http://science.howstuffworks.com/space-farming.htm Find out about research in space farming.

INDEX